Languages of the World

Swahili

Catherine Chambers

Chicago, Illinois

www.capstonepub.com
Visit our website to find out more information about Heinemann-Raintree books.

To order:
☎ Phone 888-454-2279
🖥 Visit www.capstonepub.com to browse our catalog and order online.

© 2012 Heinemann Library
an imprint of Capstone Global Library, LLC
Chicago, Illinois

Edited by Dan Nunn and Diyan Leake
Designed by Marcus Bell
Original illustrations © Capstone Global Library Ltd 2012
Picture research by Elizabeth Alexander
Originated by Capstone Global Library Ltd
Printed and bound in China by South China Printing
  Company Ltd

15 14 13 12 11
10 9 8 7 6 5 4 3 2 1

Library of Congress Cataloging-in-Publication Data

Chambers, Catherine, 1954-
  Swahili / Catherine Chambers.—1st ed.
    p. cm.—(Languages of the world)
  Includes bibliographical references and index.
  ISBN 978-1-4329-5838-1—ISBN 978-1-4329-5846-6 (pbk.)
1. Swahili language—Textbooks for foreign speakers—English.
2. Swahili language—Grammar. 3. Swahili language—Spoken
Swahili. I. Title. II. Series: Languages of the world (Chicago,
Ill.)
  PL8702C43 2012
  496'.39282421—dc23   0872   2011017927

Acknowledgments
The author and publishers are grateful to the following for permission to reproduce copyright material: Alamy pp. 7 (© dbimages), 13 (© National Geographic Image Collection), 14 (© blickwinkel), 15 (© Karin Duthie), 17 (© Jake Lyell), 19 (© Charlotte Thege), 20 (© Picture Contact BV), 23 (© Yadid Levy), 24 (© dbimages), 26 (© blickwinkel), 27 (© Karin Duthie), 29 (© Alex Bramwell); Corbis pp. 12 (© Kristian Buus/In Pictures), 21 (© Wendy Stone), 25 (© Wendy Stone); Dreamstime.com pp. 9 (© Danijel Micka), 18 (© Komela); Photolibrary pp. 6 (Frédéric Soreau), 8 (Sébastien Boisse/Photononstop), 16 (Rieger Bertrand); Photoshot p. 28 (EPA/Kim Ludbrook); Shutterstock pp. 5 (© haider), 10 (© discpicture), 11 (© AlexGul), 22 (© Attila Jandi).

Cover photograph of a boy from the Great Rift Valley, Kenya, Africa, reproduced with permission of Photolibrary (Keith Levit Photography).

Every effort has been made to contact copyright holders of material reproduced in this book. Any omissions will be rectified in subsequent printings if notice is given to the publisher.

Disclaimer
All the Internet addresses (URLs) given in this book were valid at the time of going to press. However, due to the dynamic nature of the Internet, some addresses may have changed, or sites may have changed or ceased to exist since publication. While the author and publisher regret any inconvenience this may cause readers, no responsibility for any such changes can be accepted by either the author or the publisher.

Contents

Swahili words in this book are in italics, *like this*.
You can find out how to say them by looking in the
pronunciation guide.

Swahili Around the World

Swahili is a language that began on the eastern coast of Africa. People first spoke Swahili over 1,000 years ago. Since then, Swahili has spread through East and Central Africa.

This maps shows the parts of Africa where Swahili is spoken.

Boats like these took goods and the Swahili language far and wide.

Over hundreds of years, more people began to speak Swahili. Swahili was spread further by the British and the Germans, who once ruled East African countries.

Who Speaks Swahili?

About 100 million people speak Swahili in East, Central, and Southern Africa. The Waswahili people speak Swahili as their first language. Other people speak it as a second language. This means that they also speak another language at home.

This family from Tanzania speaks three languages: Swahili, English, and Chaga.

HAKUNA MATATA!

Most people in East and Central Africa understand Swahili posters.

The proper word for Swahili is *Kiswahili*. There are many kinds of Swahili. Kimvita is spoken in the city of Mombasa in Kenya. Kiunguja is Swahili spoken on Zanzibar island. Zanzibar is part of Tanzania.

Swahili and English

Most Swahili words come from local languages spoken along the East African coast. Many words come from Arabic. Some come from Persian and a few come from other languages. Words such as *skuli* (school) and *daktari* (doctor) came from English.

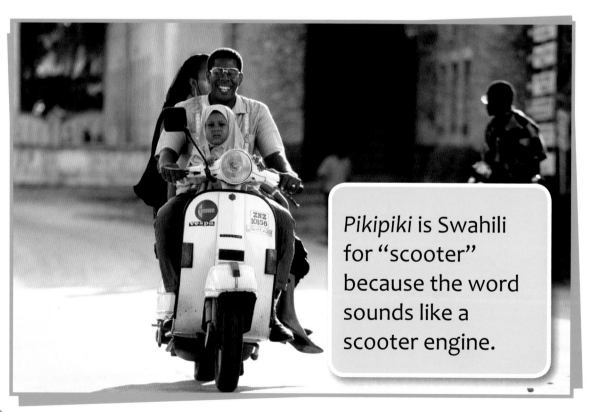

Pikipiki is Swahili for "scooter" because the word sounds like a scooter engine.

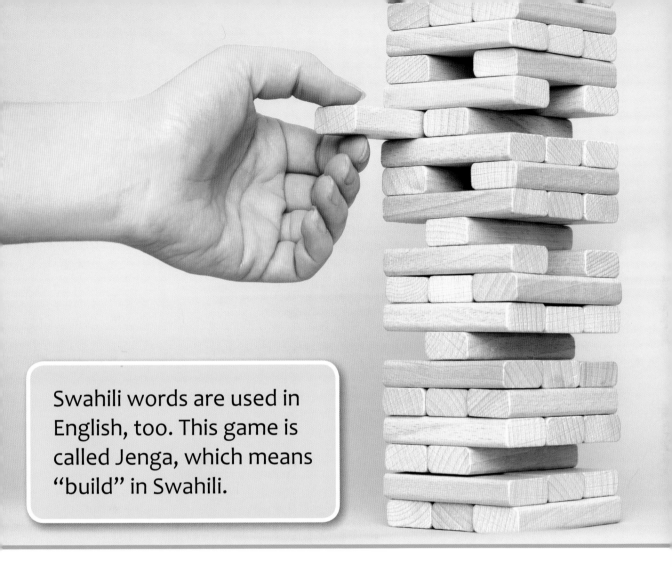

Swahili words are used in English, too. This game is called Jenga, which means "build" in Swahili.

Swahili is always changing. Young people in Nairobi, Kenya's capital city, speak Sheng. Sheng is a mixture mostly of Swahili and English. *Tichee* is "teacher" and *makoo* is "market" in Sheng.

Learning Swahili

Long ago, Swahili was written only in Arabic writing. Now, Swahili is written like English. There are 24 main letters or sounds used in the alphabet.

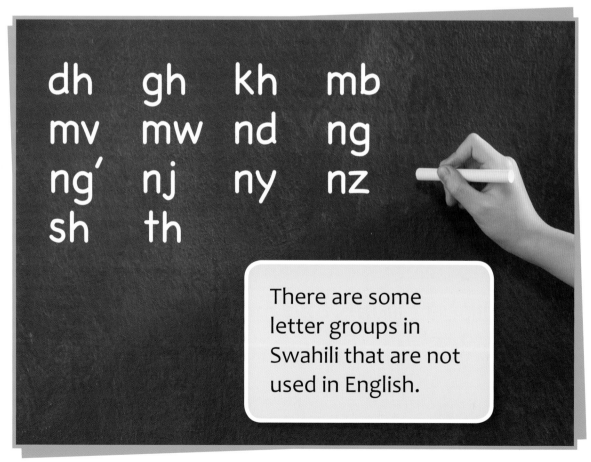

dh   gh   kh   mb
mv   mw   nd   ng
ng´ nj   ny   nz
sh   th

There are some letter groups in Swahili that are not used in English.

Swahili has some very long words. For example, *Amekiandika* means, "He (or she) has written it." Swahili has no "he" or "she" words. It also has no words for "a" or "the."

Saying Hello and Goodbye

Most Swahili-speakers just smile when they meet. Some shake or lightly touch hands. We might say, "Hi!" Some people say, "*Hujambo!*" The other person replies, "*Sijambo!*"

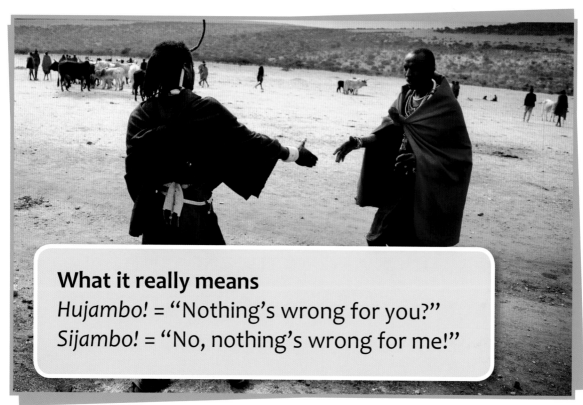

What it really means
Hujambo! = "Nothing's wrong for you?"
Sijambo! = "No, nothing's wrong for me!"

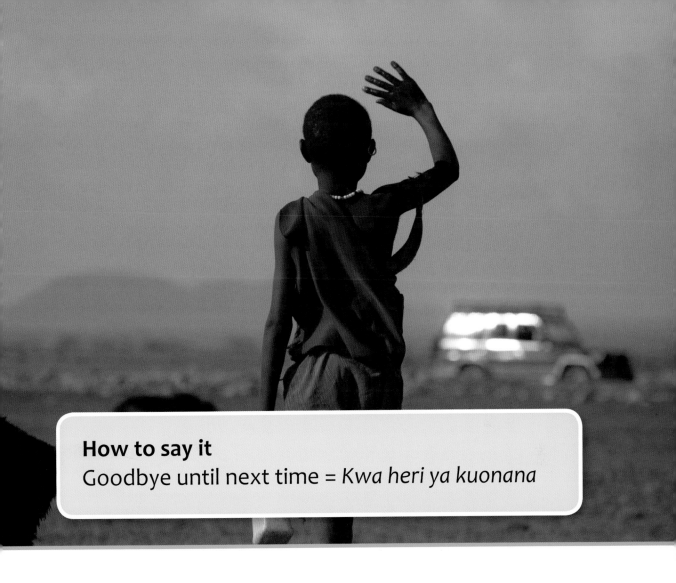

You say, "*Kwa heri*" when you leave someone. It means "With blessing." When you leave more than one person, you say, "*Kwa herini.*" In English, we would just say, "Goodbye."

Talking About Yourself

When you meet people for the first time, they may ask you what your name is. To tell someone your name, you can say, "*Jina langu ...*" ("My name is ...").

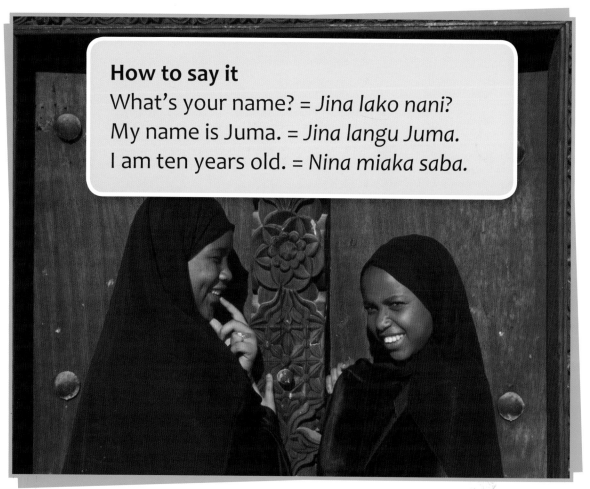

How to say it
What's your name? = *Jina lako nani?*
My name is Juma. = *Jina langu Juma.*
I am ten years old. = *Nina miaka saba.*

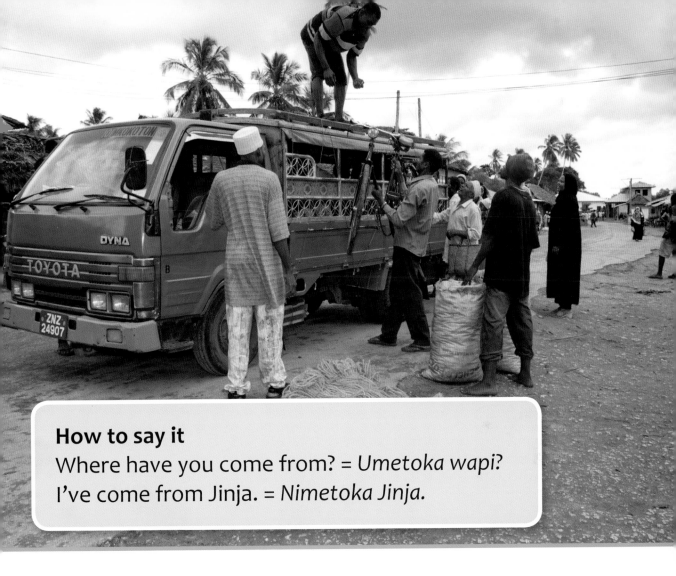

How to say it

Where have you come from? = *Umetoka wapi?*

I've come from Jinja. = *Nimetoka Jinja.*

New people arrive in Africa's large towns and cities every day. They move there to work. People might ask where they come from and where they live.

Asking About Others

You can ask many questions beginning with the words *"Habari za ...?"* ("How is ...?" or "How are ...?") The answer to many questions might be *"Nzuri"* ("Fine"). You can explain afterward if things are bad, though!

How to say it
How's your new bicycle? = *Habari za baisikeli mpya?*

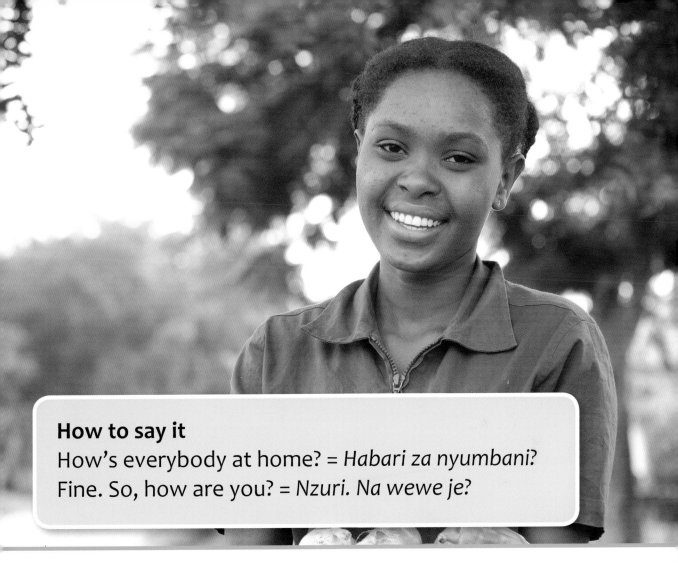

How to say it
How's everybody at home? = *Habari za nyumbani?*
Fine. So, how are you? = *Nzuri. Na wewe je?*

It is important to ask if people are well and happy. In Swahili, it is polite to ask about the whole family. You can do this by using the word *nyumbani*, which means "at home."

At Home

In the old cities on the coast of East Africa, there are stone houses and concrete skyscrapers. In the countryside, houses are made of wooden poles and clay, or cement blocks.

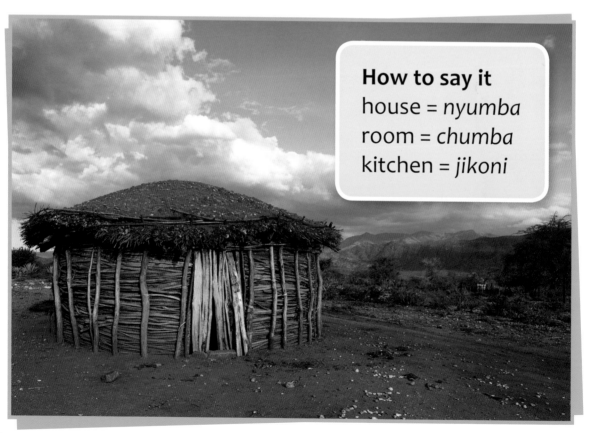

How to say it
house = *nyumba*
room = *chumba*
kitchen = *jikoni*

How to say it
garden = *bustani*
tree = *mti*
inner courtyard = *behewa*

Thick walls and small windows keep
out the heat in stone and clay homes.
Families often sit in cool courtyards or
under shady trees outside.

Families

Families can be quite large. Grandparents live with their children and grandchildren. Aunts and uncles live nearby. Families are often smaller in the modern cities.

How to say it
mom = *mama*
dad = *baba*
aunt = *shangazi*
uncle = *mjomba, amu,* or *ami*

Brothers, sisters, cousins, and friends all might call each other *ndugu*!

Brothers and sisters are both called *ndugu*. *Ndugu mume* or *ndugu wa kiume* is a brother. *Ndugu mke* or *ndugu wa kike* is a sister.

Having Fun

Children like to listen to music and hang out. Sometimes they play singing games by tapping sticks together or clapping. Many listen to Swahili rap, too. People are crazy about soccer and basketball!

How to say it
soccer = *mpira or soka*
I'm playing soccer = *Nacheza mpira*
song = *wimbo*
I'm singing = *Naimba*

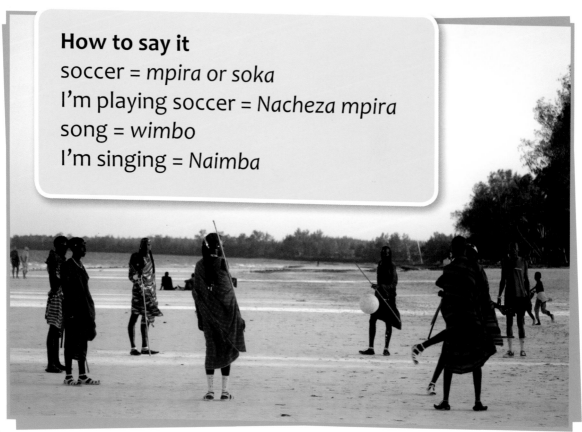

How to say it
I'm playing bao = *Nacheza bao*

Bao is a traditional board game that spread from the East African islands hundreds of years ago. Beginners enjoy playing bao, but it is a serious game, like chess. Experts play in competitions.

23

At School

School days start early in East Africa. School children have a school uniform. Most walk to school. They make sure their classrooms and playground are clean and neat.

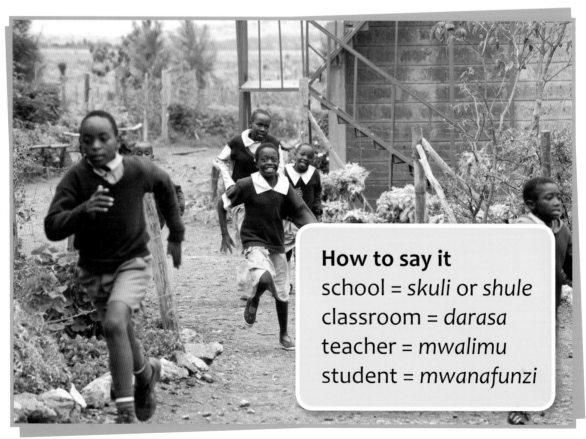

How to say it
school = *skuli* or *shule*
classroom = *darasa*
teacher = *mwalimu*
student = *mwanafunzi*

How to say it
numbers = *hesabu*

In East Africa, most students learn both
Swahili and English. They learn subjects
such as history, geography, and math.
They also learn about staying healthy
and taking care of the environment.

Food and Drink

Maize (corn), rice, vegetables, and many types of bean are popular in parts of East and Central Africa. They eat fresh fish and fruits such as mangoes and bananas, too. You can find burgers and fries in the big cities.

How to say it
food = *chakula*
cooked maize = *ugali*
cooked rice = *wali*
beans = *maharagwe*
fish = *samaki*
banana = *ndizi*

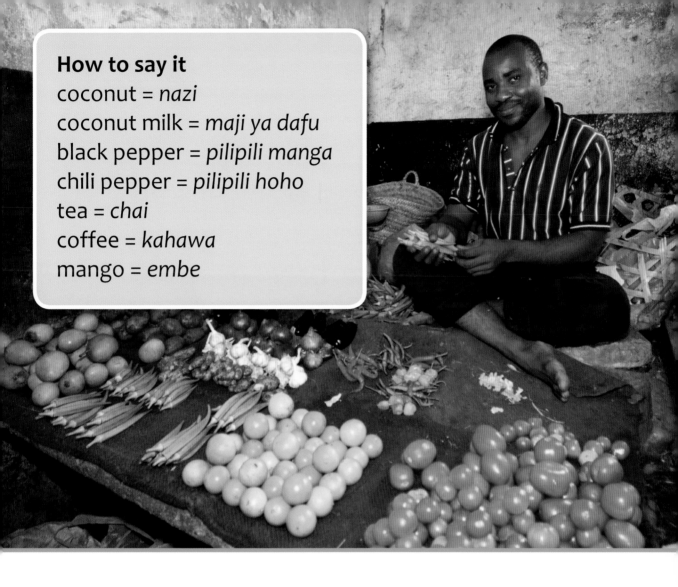

Spices and coconuts add flavor to food. They grow well on the islands off the East African coast. Tea and coffee are popular. They grow on bushes in East and Central Africa.

Clothes

Farmers in East and Central Africa grow cotton to make clothes. Many Africans wear a dress shirt and pants or a skirt if they work in an office, bank, or school. They wear jeans and T-shirts when they are relaxing.

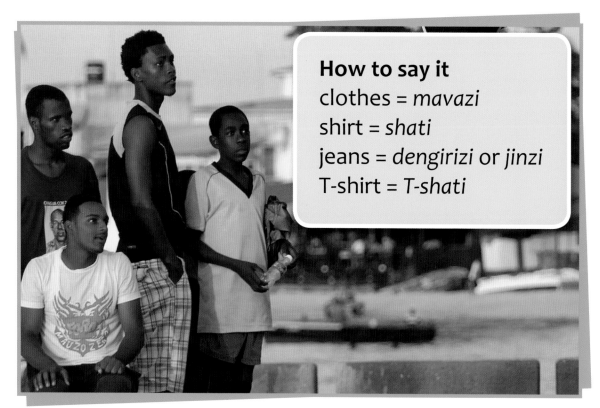

How to say it
clothes = *mavazi*
shirt = *shati*
jeans = *dengirizi* or *jinzi*
T-shirt = *T-shati*

How to say it
skirt cloth = *kanga*
long gown = *kanzu*
man's cloth = *kikoi*

Many women wear patterned cloths that are tied to make skirts. Some men wear long cotton gowns, or cloths wrapped around their waists. Patterns and colors of the cloth change over time.

Pronunciation Guide

English	Swahili	Pronunciation
aunt	*shangazi*	*shaan-**gah**-zee*
banana	*ndizi*	*nn-**dee**-zee*
beans	*maharagwe*	*maa-haa-**rahg**-way*
bicycle	*baisikeli*	*by-sih-**kel**-ee*
brother	*ndugu wa kiume*	*nn-**doo**-goo wa kee-**oo**-may*
	ndugu wa kike	*nn-**doo**-goo wa **kee**-kay*
build	*jenga*	***jeng**-ga*
chili pepper	*pilipili hoho*	***pee**-lee **pee**-lee **ho**-ho*
classroom	*darasa*	*da-**rah**-sa*
cloth (men's)	*kikoi*	***kee**-koi*
cloth (women's)	*kanga*	***kahng**-ga*
coconut	*nazi*	***nah**-zee*
coconut milk	*maji ya dafu*	***mah**-jee ya da-**foo***
coffee	*kahawa*	*ka-**haa**-wa*
courtyard	*behewa*	*be-**hay**-wa*
dad	*baba*	***baa**-ba*
fine/good	*nzuri*	*nn-**zoo**-ree*
fish	*samaki*	*sa-**mah**-kee*
food	*chakula*	*cha-**koo**-la*
garden	*bustani*	*boos-**tah**-nee*
goodbye	*kwa heri* (to one person)	*kwa-**hey**-ree*
	kwa herini (to more than one)	*kwa-hey-**ree**-nee*
gown (long)	*kanzu*	***kaan**-zoo*
hello	*hujambo/sijambo* (in reply)	*hoo-**jahm**-bo/see-**jahm**-bo*

house	*nyumba*	**nyoom**-ba
How is ...?	*Habari za ...?*	ha-**baa**-ree **zaa**
I'm playing ...	*Nacheza*	na-**chee**-za
in the house/at home	*nyumbani*	nyoom-**bah**-nee
I've come from ...	*Nimotoka ...*	nee-mee-**toh**-ka
jeans	*dengerizi/jinzi*	deng-gey-**ree**-zee/**jin**-zee
kitchen	*jikoni*	jee-**koh**-nee
mango	*embe*	**em**-bay
market	*makoo*	**mah**-koo
mom	*mama*	**maa**-ma
music	*muziki*	moo-**zee**-kee
My name is ...	*Jina langu ni ...*	jee-na lang-**goo** nee
numbers/math	*hesabu*	**hey**-sa-boo
pants (casual)	*suruali ndefu*	soo-roo-**ah**-lee nn-**dey**-foo
rice (cooked)	*wali*	**wah**-lee
room	*chumba*	**choom**-ba
school	*skuli*	**skoo**-lee
shirt	*shati*	**shah**-tee
soccer	*mpira/soka*	mm-**pee**-ra/**sok**-ka
student	*mwanafunzi*	mwah-na-**foon**-zee
tea	*chai*	**chi** (rhymes with "eye")
teacher	*mwalimu*	mwa-**lee**-moo
tree	*mti*	mm-**tee**
T-shirt	*T-shati*	**tee**-shah-tee
uncle	*mjomba/amu/ami*	mm-**jom**-ba/**ah**-moo **ah**-mee
water	*maji*	**mah**-jee
Where have you come from?	*Umatoka wapi?*	oo-ma-**toh**-ka **wah**-pee
years	*miaka*	mee-**ah**-ka

1 = *moja*, 2 = *mbili*, 3 = *tatu*, 4 = *nne*, 5 = *tano*, 6 = *sita*, 7 = *saba*, 8 = *nane*, 9 = *tisa*, 10 = *kumi*

Find Out More

Books

Feelings, Muriel. *Jambo Means Hello: Swahili Alphabet Book.* Logan, Iowa: Perfection Learning, 2009.

Feelings, Muriel. *Moja Means One: Swahili Counting Book.* Logan, Iowa: Perfection Learning, 2006.

Knight, Margy Burns. *Africa Is Not a Country.* Brookfield, Conn.: Millbrook, 2002.

Krebs, Laurie, and Julia Cairns. *We All Went on Safari: A Counting Journey Through Tanzania.* Cambridge, Mass.: Barefoot, 2004.

Websites

www.swahili4kids.com

Index

MAY   2012